MACHU PICCHU ME

Carlos Hiraldo

Palamedes
San Francisco

Copyright © 2016 by Carlos Hiraldo
All Rights Reserved

Palamedes Publishing
www.palamedes.pub
San Francisco

Cover by Kate Marchio
www.katemarchiophotography.com

ISBN 978-0-692-47720-5
LCCN 2016903771

Also available in ebook:
Kindle 770c93ca-c4ae-480c-a54b-57fae0872e74
EPUB 08f57d1a-60e2-4640-85ff-a03c985b14be
www.palamedes.pub/books/machu-picchu-me

www.facebook.com/PalamedesPub
www.twitter.com/PalamedesPub

The poems in this collection were written from 1993 to 2007.

"Machu Picchu Me," "Santo Domingo," "From My Ghetto," "Mullaney and Me," "Coco," "Latino Be-Gunned" and "First Night" first appeared from 1996 to 1998 in *Snark: A Journal of Poetry & Translations*.

"Machu Picchu Me," "On the Uptown Platform," "Despertar," "Flash Gordon Poet," "From My Ghetto," and "Kate Winslet" appeared online in *Clickable Poems*.

"Smile" appeared in the journal *Struggle*, Volume 17, Number 2 in 2001.

"How Fat You Are" and "Santo Domingo" appeared in *The Bilingual Review: A Journal of Arizona State University*, Volume XXVI, Number 1, January-April, 2001-2002.

"St. Nicholas Avenue" and "This Is Not a Poem, Much Less a Love One" appeared in *Fire*, Number 18 in September 2002.

"Kate Winslet" also appeared in *Other Poetry*, Series II, Number 21 in the winter of 2003.

"On the Court," "Thank You Brittany Woods," and "Barry Bonds" appeared online in *TimbookTu*.

"Discovery" appeared in *Taj Mahal Review* in 2003.

"Cosmic" appeared in *Voyages: An Anthology of World Poetry* in 2003.

"No Suicides" appeared online in *3rd Muse Poetry Journal*, Issue # 30, April-June 2005.

"Papi" appeared in *Our Truth: A Forthright Poetry Compilation* in the fall of 2005.

"Off Sylvia Plath" appeared in *Still Standen: A Celebration of the Poet's Life* in 2007.

for Emma (1935-2002), mami

Earth 1

Machu Picchu Me	2
Santo Domingo	4
Papi	5
Sosua	7
Mullaney and Me	8
Father Toys	9
Latino Be-Gunned	11
Partition	13
Coco	14
Off Sylvia Plath	15

Stone 17

The Abortions	18
On the Court	19
Our Human Suffering	22
It's Good to Me	24
On the Uptown Platform	26
How Fat You Are	28
St. Nicholas Avenue	31

Rachel Weisz	34
Despertar	36
Flash Gordon Poet	39
From My Ghetto	42

Sky 43

This Is Not a Poem, Much Less a Love One	44
Kate Winslet	46
Thank You Brittany Woods	48
Smile	50
Discovery	52
From the Bushdocter Café	53
No Suicides	55
Barry Bonds	57
Cosmic	59
Fall	61
Forever	62
First Night	64
Higher	65

Acknowledgements 72

About the Author 74

Earth

Machu Picchu Me

I write poems
because without them
I would just be weird,
because I hope to be put down now
and have my corpse found
on mountain heights
where flowers grow freely,
because no one could be so blind
to ask a flower
to hide its color,
because a private collection of poems
is merely a journal to me,
and a journal is the encasement
of a muted soul,
because diary entries
like dairy products
turn sour
once their moment has expired,
because I cannot
keep myself to myself,
because like a Peruvian
discovering his Inca empire,
my introspection

must be more than personal,
because I must leave
a stone solid edifice
redeeming my existence
from the arbitrary moment,
like an Incan temple
rising to the heavens
while Pizarro's shiny loot
lies obscure
under anonymous earth,
because my poems
are to be ruins of my emotions
that may serve
beyond their momentary origins
to become sources of knowledge
or, at least, tourist attractions.

Santo Domingo

If Africa begins at the Pyrenees,
then it ends here,
where waves crash on sands
like unwelcomed galleons,
where winds hit palm trees
the way wars and conquests have bent
beautiful brown people,
who boast ugly about the first cathedral in the Americas,
where a pile of dusty bones claims it is Columbus buried,
who complain about the need to expel Haitians
as they risk sanity, health, and dignity
on wooden rafts to dollared Puerto Rico,
and turn their backs on Enriquillo,
a man who once sacrificed health for sanity and dignity
to warn natives in Cuba of impending Conquistadors,
and just before burning at the stake
refused conversion
lest his soul spend eternity in a heaven full of Spaniards
and his body back in Santo Domingo with a rotting Columbus.

Papi

You followed the hot river of your favorite whiskey;
teeth first,
then lips,
chin
and eyes,
blinded by the hollow darkness down your esophagus.

There went your brains.
Then your callous hands that worked hard since 12 in
    Dominican fields,
that held the steering wheels
of your death-defying 1970s Washington Heights livery cars,
that caressed mom, that beat her and my sister,
that squeezed my lips affectionately,
that wrote letters to your relatives
arguing I was too black and *bembú* to be your offspring.

Dark brown hands that delivered the chocolate Mr. Softee cone
to my toddler mouth, that delivered the whiskey
through your numbed, old lips, down to your bloated liver.
Everything going down with the favorite poison;
eyes,
ears,

nose,
hands,
heart,
kisses, caresses,
Sssswwoooooopppp! and a bloated liver
blowing up Ppllooowww!
into nada.

Sosua

Tonight I'm OK.

Only a few hours ago the beach was packed
with a multitude of different shades;
Caucasian tourists, brown folks getting blacker,
blonde beauty queens frolicking with muscular Haitians,
crowds of Creoles glaring in disdain
and American couples discovering a lost paradise.

But tonight everything is clear.
The starry sky provides enough light
to comfortably close my eyes
and listen to the moon have its way with the ocean
and feel the breeze do the same to my hair.

Why should I be surprised to be back here
and, much less, to find myself at peace?

Mullaney and Me

The night before at MA's
you stated, "I think I am,"
when responding to my despairing,
"Between that Oreo and Malcolm X,
there's got to be a middle ground."

Sunny suburban morning at BC passing you by,
Wednesday's limp after Tuesday's spirit flight.
Orphans of urbia, phantoms
crashing through your city soul.
Did you miss the parade of pretty intelligent looking blondes
smiling in company of L.L. Bean shirts?

A sagging bag, a downward cast,
your white face looking like it had something to say.
Dirty spaghetti hair under sweaty cap,
blue "Bronx Bombers" T-shirt faded off-white,
your ripped jeans more torn than the rest,
and the scratch and the scrape of mud-brown shit-kickers
on the careless gravel of an expensively packed parking lot
gave a blue-collar dignity to your slumbering walk.

Father Toys

Five-six Dominican giant,
bringing toys and temper to an anxious homestead.

Beer brown globe belly
from where—sitting on your lap,
sharing your Schaefer— we would trace
Columbus's passage to the new world.
America, your tired world—
a raggedy used livery car
every year,
still trailing years behind.

Catching up with the anger from your whip,
you'd chase Zuly and me,
distributing your arbitrary justice,
breaking skin
for broken toys.

And after the storm,
the calm organizing of dollar bills
on your bed.
You would drool for dead Presidents
that would soon abandon you,

a lusting masturbator in a peep-show.

As we hesitated at your door,
you'd throw a retreating side glance.
You'd bribe your conscience, giving us a choice,
the Jaws set or
the battered Funny Bone doctor kit.
Fearing further pain from the jagged mouth
of the grey fish
and shunning responsibility
for the red-nosed patient,
we trusted the old stand-by,
a broken TV set kept in your room.
We would sit behind it,
steering the round UHF antenna—
a temporary getaway car.

Latino Be-Gunned*

Are you sick of little, unwanted guests?
Are you tired of stepping into pesky Mexicans
everywhere you go?
Have the loud boom-box Dominicans
outside your window
kept you up for yet another night?
Has the grass in your favorite park been trampled
by all kinds of soccer-playing South Americans?
Don't get angry.
Don't use ineffective fly swatters
that don't perform on larger insects.
Don't buy roach motels that only house part of the problem.
Don't use traditional sprays that only kill the visible Latinos.
Use the power spray that works.
Use the power spray that kills & sterilizes survivors.
Use "Latino Be-Gunned"
& watch your insect problems disappear.
Pay just $10.98 for a can today
& soon you'll have cleaner streets, prettier gardens,
& you'll be able to enjoy the sound sleep
that comes with the peace of mind
of a clean & safe environment.

Remember, "With Latino Be-Gunned Greasers are Done."

Not to be ingested. Keep away from small children. If family members experience irritation to eyes and/or skin, discontinue use immediately.

Partition

Papi's car won't start today.
He won't make the suits' early raise.
Today, he ain't getting paid.

I can remember better scenes.
Late crawls to his sparse bed,
where I thought I could safely dream.

And in early hours, I'd return,
my time tossing and bargaining spent.
I'd return to my mother's concerns.

Mornings he'd finish his warm beer
breakfast, giving him energy to overcome
the bitter paralysis behind the gear.

Papi's car sits parked today.
Like dirty urban trees, blood and syringe,
part of the neighborhood scene.

Coco

I'm the coconut shaking loose from the clutching palm.
The wind helps when it wants
and when the weather stays dead calm,
the wrinkled black man jams his toes on the trunk.

The tropical sun safely nourishes native skins
braiding yellow hairs on the sand.
The tropical sun that ripened
now bids me die.

I heed the call,
no longer ashamed of my form.
My hard brown shell may reveal
the mushy whiteness so long concealed.

Let me fall the long distance,
the soft white sands will embrace,
the dirt-rusty machete will liberate
my tasty, bittersweet juice.

Off Sylvia Plath

What's so special about my rotting teeth anyway?
Everyone has a dentist or a priest they avoid.

I can't flick a cigarette butt in your face to realize I'm alive
or pat a co-ed on the behind
to have something new to say.
If I'd grab a white by the lapel
and yell, "What the fuck is wrong with you! Do you know
    what's wrong with you!"
there would be something wrong with me, even if I just wrote
    about that
to smack a ghost of what I could've been.

Washington Heights was my loud, sweaty, dirty, *oye-papi*
    muse,
making me point out what everyone noticed quietly.

But the old hood is now full of Starbucks and nice, young,
    interracial couples.

Just because I wanted my love to last forever,
doesn't mean its poem should.

Here, the red red rose smells like old cheese and rain drops on
   the air conditioner sound like tin, Rin Tin Tin,
though no dogs bark in quiet Sunnyside.

People are out, but no one's around.

I want to explode into you.
I just need a new fuse, a stronger match, a better light, an
   apple-pie.

Stone

The Abortions

A blessing for the abortions.
A blood clot dripping in toilet water,
a marriage ended at the second date,
the romance stunted to friendship,
the silence,
the gaze in a subway car,
a new girlfriend with two previous kids,
the pet cat licking my palms,
Al-Qaeda bombed in the mountains,
and the poem cut mercifully short.

On the Court

Blondie
take me into you
and I'll take ya
outta your world.
Blondie
you make me
wanna talk to ya in slang
open doors for ya and pat
you on the behind
as you walk on by.

Blondie
let me kiss your cheeks
as you make yourself
in the mirror,
take a glance and admire
your face
and my sweet-nigga smile.

Blondie
let me hug and hold ya,
whisper in your ears
how

I wanna fuck ya,
I wanna fuck up Ghandi.
Light a light
for my black soul
Blondie.

Tell me "no,"
with a soft soul smile.
Tell me to behave
or I won't get any,
let me convince ya,
let me hear ya say yes
to loving ya,
let me be
the nigga that rapes
just by being
here
in our marriage bed.

Blondie
let me kill ya,
keep our children
in the dark,
with a hand in their pants
and a shuffle in their steps.

Let the world
make them love ya
with a distance,
let the world
make them love me
with hate
at what I done
made us do

the World

all over again.

Our Human Suffering

for Vanesa

It hurts to miss your face
for three days. It hurts to imagine you
there smoking, drinking coffee,
mornings in front of your computer,
leathering your skin,
killing yourself with every puff,
like we stab our love in the back
with every nasty word we lash out.

Our arms reach out for a hug
through massive walls of concrete,
laid brick by brick with experience;
our spic mothers' hands crashing out,
a porcelain plate over your head,
a ring quickly retreating
from my bloodied mouth,
our immigrant fathers
gone the long hours
in search of America's promise.

You waited every night
for his return from his store.
I dreaded his return every night
with liquor and violence.
Our families, a divergence of dysfunction,
your immigrant Jewish success surrendered by Latinness,
my family's failings, the explainable
experience of self-hating *négros*. Our
distorted faces meet here, arrowed
screams calling through years
of butchered ancestors in pogroms, lynchings,
middle passages, and hot ovens. Our attraction,
our love, our fear, the past now calling us forth to hurt
each other till death do us part
in the name of the
Aryan, the master race, the shylock, the zambo,
our Juan Valdez, the father, the son, and the holy spirit of love,
Amen.

It's Good to Me

The cops don't walk like cops in Amsterdam
—they walk like bureaucrats,
black-hatted, short white sleeves,
razor thin black ties, slick grey slacks,
rail thin men and women scurry
through narrow streets
forgetful of their guns,
like office drones
hurrying to pick up paper piles.

The cops don't walk like cops in Amsterdam
—they walk like bureaucrats,
which is good to me
when I stumble into one of them
in a pot haze.

The cops don't walk like cops in Amsterdam
—they walk like bureaucrats,
which is good to me
when one follows my wizz…dumb against the wall
in Annefrankenstraadt
as I go next to the overflowing street urinal,
peeing away pot, dignity, and time.

Which is good to me.

On the Uptown Platform

My apologies. I think.
Don't give me that dirty look.
You could now be mistaken
for one of those *tan* gringas
I saw on the brown beaches
of Santo Domingo
cavorting with
coal-black brothers.

After I so lightly touched
your yellow hair,
I should've offered
to assemble
those soft boiled
spaghetti strings
into corn rows.

Believe me,
my ivory señorita,
it was an accident.
I was only pointing out
to my man Julio
the big Calvin Klein bill board

of little Kate Moss.
What I said to him was,
"*Ella necesita más.*"
Nothing, nothing about nice ass.

How Fat You Are

In America,
the rich get richer
and the poor get fatter.
No need to go about much
to see the ugliness
of the neighborhood.
With little money
and lots of time,
there are lots of choices
for greasy food
and the stationary travel
of the television
that can bring
all the beauty of life
into the apartment's living room
or the back door
of the trailer home.
Burgers and bad sitcoms,
cheap pizza pies
and football games
with piss-water beer
to fill up the empty times,
the arteries and egos.

Soon you'll believe
you look like the partner
of the beautiful model
smiling in the Coors commercial,
though you've never been skiing
and would have a heart attack
if you tried.

President Truman
kept his health
with a sparing diet
and brisk morning walks
through Washington D.C.
like Balaguer did
through Santo Domingo
after more than
50 years
of public life
in that Caribbean land.
His minimalist diet
of boiled chicken, plantains
and cabbages
kept him going
despite his blindness.

Now-a-days
in the third world
the ideal of fat
is a thing of the poor.
Only they
still greet you at the door
with earnest smiles
on their dark faces and
"Oh, how fat you are!"
as the highest compliment.

St. Nicholas Avenue

I
wouldn't raise a hand
to turn back
the clock's hand.
I
wouldn't get up
and walk away
from this moment,
lying here in bed,
sleepless
with thoughts of the years past
and the fear
of more like that
to come.

Dominicans love
lukewarm spring or fall nights
in Washington Heights,
with loud Merengue
blaring from open windows.
The guira, like a bottle-cap
scratching on concrete,
a cheese grinder and a pick,

the practical musical
instruments of slaves.

Whites can ignore
the noise, the music,
the sirens running
here to there
with no seeming purpose
but to wail.
Whites can pretend
to sleep,
knowing they're just passing by
toward
Columbia Medical School
or temporary poverty.

I
lie here,
closing and opening my eyes,
as the noise
wanes and starts up,
opening and closing my eyes,
exchanging one darkness
for another,
thinking of my childhood here,

and in Santo Domingo,
my college years in Boston
and Long Island.
My love turned to hate
turned to regret.

And I
do not move,
knowing that would mean
exchanging one darkness
for another.
You can take
the Dominican out of Washington Heights,
but the brown-American
will always be asked,
"where are you from?"

Rachel Weisz

I wanna spin my words and lines like a magic dreidl
twirl, twirl, twirling 5000 years round the world,
onboard satellites, spinning around attention,
'cause all movements cause suspicion.
Mami, look at those big, dark eyes—Dare I say
you own the world?
Run the media? Gather elders to plan the World Bank under
    Waspish approval?
Who cares? Let me smell your thick hair and caress your
    almond face.
Let me face what I can't face. There, I say you can run
my world.
Look me up in my US ghetto.
They rent me a tenement, roach infested apartment,
which you call in your British accent "flat." Thick black girls
    will call me a "trheydor"
in their thick Latin accents.
Recall Krakow in '43. Come join me
to be hated, together, in tight embrace
of the hate that hates us both. Our self-hate will overflow into
    each other's cup.

While we wait for doom, blow me a kiss from your Bantu lips,
> hook me with your hooked Mediterranean nose, Caesar
> breathes easier now,

while I bite your big, elegant ears. I get in gear to soil that
> knowing whiteness.

This black rapist will leave the blonde virgins alone.

Despertar

for Michelle

Come on
my little Asian girl
come on
let the nigga in you out
we all got the nigga inside
some of us are the nigga,
but we all got the nigga inside—
let's stop watching the hours fall
like swatted roaches from a white wall
let the nigga in you shine
put the book down
snuff out the bong
put the book down
and listen to the crowds
on your street,
West 4th Street,
any street,
it doesn't matter
keep the beat
to the different feet
the sweat and the blood

the smell of laughter
after a hard day's work
on the road, in the factory,
the police-station, the streets
coming home
to music
to rest and relax
all coming home to sit
and unwind
here,
all coming home
back to you
here
with our bongs
and our books
and our booked conversation
about the pain of the office
which is the pain of no pain
while you're living,
the pain of listening to the streets
but not walking among the crowds,
the pain of the soul as a resting place,
the tomb is our final home,
not the carriage there.
So snuff out the bong,

put the book down
my little Asian girl
and walk on out
to the streets
where all the niggas are out.

Flash Gordon Poet

for Erik

Flash Gordon
writer, lover
poet,
quick burnout,
so high
the next thing I do
is like the next thing I do
and the first thing I've ever done,
quick burn out
PhD high
Flash Gordon poet
high on speed
before the low
of tomorrow's
office
labor
PhD high—
low
unemployed thinker
like today's toy
soldier

stepped into different
shades of darkness
from blonde to black
all leading
to success
in the brain
poet or loser,
drunkard or genius
questions
all leading to success,
smooth, flattened
low
by my hand
evened
by my hand
like the road behind me,
from ghetto to grass
to academe,
and the road ahead will be
like the next thing I do
Flash Gordon poet
by my hand
the next thing I do
leading to success
by my hand

the
end.

Do the insane sleep?
Yes, they do.
But do they get sane
when they wake up?
They sometimes do,
yes.

From My Ghetto

Fragments,
once sheltered someone.
Anonymous pebbles,
I kick clear today.

These you may read.
White chocolate, sticky caramel
on pink cotton bed sheets.
Open wrapper in an empty wastebasket.

Butterfly wings on a red rose petal.
Your white fingers fluttering,
caressing the skin of my penis.
A barren, dried stem.

An insect seeks pollen from weed.
My yellow rain fertilizes the shrubs,
another puddle rises from the gutter.
The saddest poems are on cement.

Sky

This Is Not a Poem, Much Less a Love One

for Kelly

Getting to know you
is like reading a good poem,
like negotiating life itself,
only clear in hindsight.
I'm confused now.

I'm getting to know you.
This is just a step
with many steps before
and many steps to come
to an unknown destination,
Columbus with one foot
on the Spanish port
and another on the shipboard.

This is just me
placing
my naked sole on the mud,
another step
in getting to know you,

like my fingers pressing on the pen,
like my hands on your chin,
my lips on your cheeks,
thanking you for good
or bad
making life
a little interesting
again.

Kate Winslet

Honey,
where's the rope?
For those round hips of yours,
I'll forgive
England Wordsworth
and risk its
lynching Southern children.

How can the British sun
nourish so much life?

Green eyes so inviting,
a sharp nose
poised to stab
my nigga enthusiasm,
lips
like safety cushions
for passion,
African desire
on a European landscape,
Tintern Abbey disturbed by Kilimanjaro,
black beauty onion
on the way to the talk-show couch

to speak to Americans
in oh so proper and witty
English English.

Red head burn me
for $13.50
a couple of hours
like America's failing dream
stored in your celluloid industry,
Indians at the Smithsonian.

Thank You Brittany Woods

I turn and watch
you strapped in the child seat,
in the back of your dad's car.
Your soft, black face
lights up,
smiling at the blue MTA bus
and informing me
"buela bus driver."
You get to the point,
like when you want pizza
you say, "I want pizza,"
and gently correct me
"I'm baby, I can't see"
when I point at your dad
in the pizzeria.
You even put up
with my adult impatience,
when I childishly say,
"You are tall. We are
thinking of the WNBA,"
you remind me
with a laugh,
"I'm baby, I'm growing."

Thank you Brittany Woods,
every time I go
to the North Bronx
your bright eyes
and light smile
counteract
the sullen masks
I usually see
in your fellow Dominican
toddlers
of Washington Heights.

Your dad
must have kept
his eyes open
when growing up here.

Smile

A family stands in the foreground
of this black and white world.
A man, work shirt and jacket,
cotton slacks, white looking, probably tan,
holds hands with an attractive, middle-aged woman,
black hair, eyes so bright
they could only be blue.
She wears a charcoal dress
that must have been purple.
Standing before her parents,
there's a little girl,
Shirley-Temple curls, hair so blonde
it looks yellow in this opaque scene.
Her dress is white,
could have been blue, perhaps pink,
but it looks as white and pure
as the pearl teeth
revealed by her dimpled smile.

Behind this family
a crowd of picnickers mingle,
some sitting on towels, some standing around.
These people are a blur, not easily distinguished

in the darkness of a forest's night.
The only figures clearly seen
are the spotlighted,
the family in the foreground,
brightened by the flash,
the bonfire in the background
lighting the hanging black man above it,
whose body so radically contorted from his head
preserves the snap of his neck
for all to see.

Discovery

Before there was industry,
there was art,
threatening mammoths
carved in mammoth ivory
and animals drawn
with their own blood
in cave walls
lit by fires
before the next hunt:
messages from 17,000 years ago,
telling us
the human animal has always sought
to eternalize his image
and I
do the sign of the cross
before biting another potato chip
and pressing the channel changer.

From the Bushdocter Café

Guns n Roses, like our lost love,
plays in the Bushdocter Café.
Use Your Illusion Too, they said
and we ended in disillusion.

I look out at sunny Amsterdam,
Renaissance houses with satellite roofs,
at every hot blonde through the window
I smile
but every puff I take
brings you

Estela Platz
with her rainbow poncho
Estela Platz
with her sunshine smile on rainy days
Estela Platz
with her gap tooth grin
Estela Platz
with her voluptuous sway
Estela Platz
with her black boots
Estela Platz

with sun glasses in cloudy Amsterdam
Estela Platz
with her tired plays
Estela Platz with her Gap
skirts
away from me.

And the beautiful passer-by,
these Aryan muñecas
in slick black grey designs,
smile at me
through a haze of dark smoke.

Someone sonnet me. Someone send me
explosions, the debris of torn words
hurled in 14 lines of iambic regularity,
scheduled rhymes, this final couplet
—American in Europe to forget.

No Suicides

for Keika

For the broken glass
and the angry father,
for the swinging belt,
the might-have-beens
and the spilled water,
for the shattered coffee table,
for the radio's extension cord
and the bleeding knee,
for love,
for the tall, blond officer
and the Puerto Rican social worker,
Ms. Moroney,
for the divorce,
for the lost country,
for the bicentennial
of my birth place
that can never be home,
for the beauty of my two lands,
for the beautiful people
who think they are ugly,
for the mornings I like

what I see in the mirror,
and the nights I don't look up,
for love,
for the smell of mami's hair
when she arrived from the factory
and each woman I've called baby
after emerging from her armpit,
for every woman that didn't love me back,
for the times I fucked up
because I didn't have the courage to leave
and the times we got it right
with just a look,
for the daughters that may never come
but I can't forget,
and the so desired baby boy
that didn't help Emma and Teofilo,
for all the mistakes,
for their little daughter in pink pajamas,
for the dolls that surround her,
for her searching look at the camera
for love.

Barry Bonds

For a human
to do
what he supposed
to do
so well
he hated.
"Oh well,
what
can I do?,"
you don't even ask
in that rich boy
voice,
hall of fame genes,
deep inside
you big black body
like a white aesthete
swallowed by Kunta Kinte,
like the baseball
(smack that white ass!)
screaming its way
into McCoby Bay—
all that splash!
of time and mind,

fat Ruth swings
in black and white,
prances fast from the box,
but you stare,
earring dangling
in Technicolor color,
you blackness there
to be tasted
chocolate,
an inspiration
to the palate
for a human
to do
what he
supposed to do
so well.

Cosmic

Loose debris
shoots
from its orbit
like Spanish canons
dispersing Taino Quisqueya
into mulatto Santo Domingo.

Loose debris
disappears
from its planetary orb
like a 19th century
Caribbean poet
writing snowy winters
in green January.

Loose debris
travels
through empty space
like young Emma
flying up the Atlantic,
searching.

Loose debris
arrives
in a vacuum
like her orphaned son
typing these lines
in rented New York City.

Fall

In the fall,
it rains leaves or crisp sunny days,
things fall down
like a loved one that leaves
and tells you go away
with courteous smiles
and unanswered phone calls.
That's how worlds end,
beautiful at their zenith,
colorful in red, orange,
greenish-yellow,
like a fever
from too much
being,
leading to the fall
like those leaves
floating to the ground,
looking all too familiar.

Forever

for Allison

In my midnight
studio,
lying in bed,
I come
to understand
what your word means.

It is long,
recalls death,
like the universe
stretching
only as far as my eyes
can see.

It is stifling,
a red brick wall,
neither asking nor demanding
but being STOP,
like the officer
who approached me
that rainy night

because I was
running from the rain,
showing me how
far I could
go,
letting me know
there's no escape
from the rain.

It comes down
like the tears of the accused,
like the judge's gavel,
like her flowing black robe
as she walks away,
leaving me with nothing
but the darkness
of the sentence
from her lips,
forever

like our kiss.

First Night

Can you read for me
where I left off
my vision?

Can you read melodiously
so I can start hearing
the music in poetry?

I've been a sweaty *platanero*
pushing an old wooden cart
filled with ideas and anger to sell.

Now I want
to climb orange groves
with bare feet and anxious mouth.

Higher

As we walked out the Banco Popular,
La Avenida Duarte
was a cross street north
away from la 30 de Mayo,
so I convinced my mother
to go with me.

Walking up the suburban street
I walked down every day
with my classmates,
the houses were blue
and brown, a few even
pink and some yellow.
Some were new to me,
but all had the same design;
large, one-level concrete,
two-car garage, a large satellite dish
on every roof, and doors closed.
Luis Dubois used to live here
when he was dating my sister. A dark-skinned laborer
re-enforcing a fence
said *hola* to my mother
as we reached the corner.

The avenue street turned to dust,
the construction fever of Santo Domingo
was in full swing
on this block.
De La Salle
was renovating for its 150th anniversary
of educating the richest
ladies and gentlemen
in Santiago de los 30 Caballeros.
I held my mother's
wrinkled, little hands
to help her negotiate
the mud tracks and chunks of concrete
that served as the street.

We stopped at the large gates. The garden
planted 17 years ago in agriculture class
was torn up, as the expansive driveway
I walked every morning and afternoon
was being repaved. My mother sighed,
"*ya nada es como antes.*"

Looking at the Haitian
workers in paint-dried jeans, sandals and
barefeet, I recalled crowds of students

in bright blue shirts and clean khaki pants,
some tan, many whites for a Caribbean scene,
most of them natives, others Spanish, Americans,
Germans and Dutch, and a sprinkle
of blacks. I met the whites
of the eyes of a worker
annoyed at my leisure
and we kept walking.

We turned on the corner
and found the side entrance open.
The campus
was larger than I remembered.
But it wouldn't be for long,
as the baseball field
was being brought in
by workers toiling on new buildings.

With my mother's encouragement,
I went in
as she stayed behind.
I walked through
the concrete
basketball court
where I would

play into the afternoon
with the sons of the rich
to delay returning to my aunt's
old, wooden house.

From the hair salon across the street,
Creed was beginning to ask
Can you take me higher?,
as I stared down at the circular benches
behind the bust of Duarte,
our lunch meeting place,
we called *La Perrera*.
Before Chris Mullaney, before Erik Pihel,
there I,
Francisco Jose, Henry Disla Elí,
Edward, Miguel, and Roberto Lión Chong,
sometimes known as *Chino*, other times as *Gordo*,
would discuss Cars, Baseball, Larry and Magic,
and the front, triangular design
of Marylo's too-tight pants.
We would plan and debate whether to grab her,
Spanish Laura or the hottest new girl after school,
knowing full well
all we would do
was play basketball,

baseball if there were enough
boys around, or go home.

I remembered Eliana and my first-ever kiss,
before six years of Allison,
before the small hot burst
of Kelly Smith,
and found it sad
that by the time
I was in school with her
she no longer talked
to her weird American cousin
on exile
from the dangers
of his native New York City.
Only the day before
my heart raced
every time my Godmother's daughters
mentioned her name.

I walked towards the building
with my old classroom.
Creed was now in full rock anthem riff.
Looking through the glass
of the dark wooden door, the green room

seemed small. The teacher's desk
was in the corner of the staged area
where students would nervously
solve a math problem
or place an accent mark on the blackboard. An oversized
red, white, and blue
Dominican flag
hung above the chair
and I tried to remember
if any teacher
had to hold it up
as he or she sat there.

The student's chairs
looked the same. But more.

I turned down the steps
back to the basketball court,
Creed's Higher
was fading
to a place
where blind men see.
As I walked towards her,
my mom had her face
pressed against the chain link fence

with a smile
as if finding someone
long lost.

Acknowledgements

The poems in *Machu Picchu Me* were written from 1993 to 2007.

    I would like to thank my late parents, Emma Llanos and Teofilo Hiraldo for the love, the drama, and the art. My mother's flights of fancy, which included El Viejo Gallo, an old rooster who would fly into New York City apartments to abduct kids who didn't shower, and her multiple redesigns of the six-wheel car, helped me appreciate the power of imagination to instruct and invigorate. My father's curse tirades, usually hurled at my mother, my sister, me or whoever was most handy, possessed Hopkins-like rhythms and inventiveness in Spanglish that I could somehow appreciate through the fear and embarrassment that permeated much of my childhood. Looking back at the above triumvirate of qualities with which my parents regaled me, I would have appreciated more stability and less drama. Still, their parenting style did provide much of the raw material for many of the poems in this collection.

    The many female friends and partners that came and went through the years were another source of raw, poetic inspiration. I thank them all. It's not just a sexual thing. All things being equal, I prefer the company of women over men.

I thank all the people—too many to name here—who provided feedback in formal and informal workshops. James Roderick Burns, Erik Pihel, and Annabel Short were especially encouraging. Rod put together much of the sequential order of this collection. Erik provided very insightful comments on several of these poems throughout the years. I will always look back fondly on our discussions of literature, politics, and women on Saturdays nights at Sidewalk Café in the East Village. Annabel Short provided perceptive commentary in my attempts to complete this book. She ignored with her usual sanity that she doesn't feature directly in any of the poems of this period because I didn't meet her until 2008, and having changed my life so thoroughly since then, she has also changed my writing style.

Thank You All.

About the Author

Carlos Hiraldo is a professor of English within the City University of New York. He is the author of *Segregated Miscegenation* (2003) and several articles dealing with issues of race and class which have appeared in journals like *About Campus*, *Asian American Law Journal*, and *Teaching English in the Two-Year College*. His poems have also appeared in *The Caribbean Writer*, Arizona State University's *Bilingual Review*, and the British journal *Other Poetry*. A lifelong New Yorker, he currently lives in Astoria, Queens with his wife and their two sons.

More Titles from Palamedes

- Erik Pihel, Manhattan, a mini-epic poem about New York City

Classic Ebooks
- Tradition Digitized: Ancient Poems in Modern Streams
- A Gathering Darkness: 13 Classic English Ghost Stories
- James Joyce, Dubliners
- James Joyce, A Portrait of the Artist as a Young Man
- Joseph Conrad, Heart of Darkness

www.ingramcontent.com/pod-product-compliance
Lightning Source LLC
Chambersburg PA
CBHW072104290426
44110CB00014B/1815